WHERE REALITY
SLEEPS AT NIGHT

New Poems

Paul Christensen

Cyberwit.net
HIG 45 Kaushambi Kunj, Kalindipuram
Allahabad - 211011 (U.P.) India
http://www.cyberwit.net
Tel: +(91) 9415091004
E-mail: info@cyberwit.net

An audio file is included with this book and is accessible through the QR code on title page.

Printed at QP.

Contents

I

THE DREAMS I HAVE

I'm on a river,
a strange, mineral-tasting
river, giving me zinc eyes
to see through matter,
to welcome the fish
into my imagination.
I'm in love again,
with the rocks below me.
The earth is trying
to grasp me in its muddy
arms, to kiss me with
worms in its mouth,
to make love to me
until I am reduced to
helpless prayers. The river
is bringing me to the edge
of reality, and beyond it
lies the impossible reaches
of magic, the domain
of silky phantoms
and the endless legs
of the jelly fish.
I have let go too far
this time, and now infinity
has asked me to dance.

AFTER THE ELECTION

It's a bitter wind
blowing from the future,
burning my face
as I open the window.

Its seeds will land
in the stiff grass
and rise slowly,
waving fists at us.

Ice storms
strip the branches
of birds lingering
at the gate of winter.

Soiled placards lie
in the dust, flags
furled and tossed
into a cobwebbed attic

What dread angel
spreads a virus
of populist rage
against democracy?

The West sinks into
the arms of Hitler's
progeny; Latin America
marches under fascist banners.

Africa devours its
future in war, and Asia
writhes in the coils
of an imperial python.

We vote our old
habits, but our wishes
drown in a tsunami
of authoritarianism.

Like a chain-link fence,
fate is bitter, and the kiss
it presses on us
is the seal of despair.

AT FIVE O'CLOCK, THE WORLD ROLLS OUT ITS ENDLESS RUG

It's fun to take a walk alone.
Your soul stays behind, preferring
to read a book and sip a cup of tea.
Out here, where the weeds
drag their saw teeth across
your legs, and the ants halt
to observe this towering interruption
to their schemes, you have
this vast array of forces
competing for air and a ray of light.

It's yours to observe, to interpret
as you like. Little dune houses,
armies carrying leaf shards
to their underworld kingdom,
gladiators on the lookout for rivals
and age-old enemies. The queen
resides in dark splendor, laying
her multitudes of offspring for
the hazy, undefined future.

All this lies sprawled around stagnant
pools, the odd tire, islands
of plastic bottles, a torn shirt
hung on a branch from the last flood.
A paradise of ruined dreams,
discarded desires, the rinds
of youth shed after first failures.

A tree bends down to whisper
to the nothing below, like some
dapper gent from another age.
A laugh rings out of the tangled
shrubs, and vanishes in its own echo.

Love once walked these twisting paths,
hands joined, feet tapping into the moist
veils of nightfall and a thin moon.
Be thankful there are broken Edens
among the rotting newspapers,
and joys once scribbled into letters
the mice have shredded.
A single daisy bobs its radiant
head to the ghosts that pass,
and offers its innocence to you
if you are lonely enough.

WHAT THE DARKNESS WON'T TELL ME

The marsh gives a little,
like an old farm-house bed.
It rattles its dead sedge
as you walk to the creek.
A bird is hiding nearby,
his back to me. The sky
drops its gray hair down
into the beginning of twilight.

Solitude has its barriers,
a leaning pale fence
that wanders along beside me.
A snail is frozen to the wood,
like a rivet lodged in a crack
of time. This is the museum
of fleeting pleas, each
left to drift on the forgetful wind.

Where a path winds
into an abandoned corn field,
I hear my mother's voice
beginning a new bed-time story.
She clears her throat and
a mouse scurries for cover
under the matted corn leaves.
Wild mallow stalks lean drily
in the gathering darkness,
as if to beckon me in too far.

WHERE REALITY SLEELPS AT NIGHT

The crevices of the heart turn
memories into pearls.
They lodge where fables
are born, where tales of
transformation move like
silvery worms in the realm
before language. Reality
has no tongue here; a tiny
mouth of experience tries
to speak, but nothing emerges.

The blood rushes into Stygian
pools of wonder, expanding
and contracting like the lungs
of sleep. Animals lay down
in the brown grass, under a snowfall
of stars burying the world
in serene ignorance.

The last garden withdraws
from consciousness, and leaves
behind the rubble of wordless questions.
No footprints mark the exodus of human feet,
only the rushes and crushed hay
remain, hoping to grow again.

CLOSELY OBSERVED THINGS

I peeled back the outer skin
of silence. It felt moist and warm,
as if a priest had held it
before me. It came down
out of the dark ceiling
and lay there without concern.

Not like a cat, more like
a breeze that had curled up
and stopped dreaming.
Nothing so soft as its silky
stillness, its anemic breath
smelling like yesterday.

I might put it in my pocket
and walk into town.
I'll sit on a bench and pretend
to be thinking, which deters
strangers from talking to you.
You might ask for money.

This tiny orb of emptiness
lay in a pocket of suspended
gravity, like a balloon
let go by an autistic child,
one playing on the beach
until the ocean curled around him.

PORTENTS OF EVIL

A man can't get his mower
started. He stands
sweating in the heat
wondering if he should buy
a new spark plug, or clean
the magneto with a brush.
He's alone, keeping vigil over the grass
withering at his feet.

The inertia folds
its rusty arms around
his waist and teaches him
how to dance. He once held
a girl under the street light
and kissed her, and let her
go again, as if time were
a book with endless pages.
He walked away
with the evening bolting
the emptiness to the sky.

After his marriage failed
and the kids followed their mom,
he taught himself to play guitar,
and to sing in the kitchen
late at night. His drink
stood on the counter
like a stagnant pond.
The fish all died,

and opportunity grew wings
and flew away.

When you waste a single day
of childhood, the future
stretches out in a bone-dry
desert. No one lives there.
The cities are bankrupt
and drowning under crime waves;
the hills sold out
to developers building suburbs.
It's hard to know which day
poisoned your life, but it hangs
like a soulless orb
somewhere in the mind.

II

THE NEWS TODAY

for Elizabeth Pollard, 1960-2024

Mrs. Pollard fell down
a sinkhole looking for her cat.
Her body shone in the cavernous
depths like a vein of iron.
She had called to her beloved
friend, Pepper, over and over,
her voice growing hoarse
in the cold Pennsylvania night.
Hundreds looked for her, calling
her name, some talking cat talk
to lure out the yellow siren
from her hiding place.

But there was no sign of life.
Nothing stirred out of its
winter sleep, not even dogs
behind high wooden fences.
The moon shone like
a search light, without a hand
to guide it to the crevices,
where her shoe lay in the mud.

Mrs. Pollard's body was
cold and hard on the packed clay
around her. The mine beneath
her corpse had closed seventy-
five years ago, leaving

hollows and dead-end vaults,
the circuitous routes of coal seams
leading down into the feral
depths of reptiles and rain forests.
She was among the ghosts
tucked away in the planet's bosom.

The search teams gave up,
the ladders folded and tied
to the roof, heavy coats hung
up in the crew cabin of the fire truck.
Another soul pawned at the grim
last stop of life. She had come
to offer love and faith in nature,
and held out a hand to darkness,
begging it to give back a beloved spirit.

Instead, her heel slipped on the sinkhole
rim, her leg buckled under her,
until she was small enough to be swallowed.
Thirty feet below, the ledges of hell began.
The damned moved in lockstep
at the turning of the next gallery,
dragging their feet toward oblivion.
The judas-cat had done its job, luring
her out of the lamp-lit nook
of her living room, pulling her away
from the stove and the tea kettle,
the apron on its nail, muffled
voices of her radio.

Come back, begged her husband,
who couldn't hold back his tears.

The phone rang but no one answered.
The street lights came on, the lisp
of shoes on the snow muttered
as they passed the porch. Darkness
unfolded its star-pierced umbrella
overhead, and the empty bed
grew into a frozen field covered
with echoes and squandered prayers.

No stone could bring her back
to life among the mourners.
A rust-belt town built on greed
and cheated labor, a line of stores
sealed up like old diaries
dusty with anecdotes
of Christmas eve, turkeys
on platters, breakfast bacon
and boiled coffee fresh from the stove.
Children's names lighter than paper
floated away on the river's foam.
And below, in a solemn pose
lay an acolyte of God's creation,
lips pursed with a cat's name.

MY UNCLE TONY

It was good to be down there
in his basement, the sour
smell of coal haunting
the bin behind us.
I watched his blunt fingers
ease the steel shaft
closer and closer to the
blade of his lathe,
eager to whittle the slug.

His mouth was loose, spittle
soaking a cigar butt hanging
from his rubbery lips.
He was a child of iron and
welder's slag, of rusty plates
hacked from hulls
at the wharf's edge. His eyes
bulged out of his illiterate head.

Curlicues of steel
peeled away like apple skin
and fell on his oily boots.
He missed the iron age,
and the death of his trade
as he squinted at his pulpy hands.
He coughed and looked up
as if I had come to fire him.

THE EDUCATION OF THE SOUL

The front door is a fragile
barrier between the
platitudes of the street,
and the melting logic
of the couch in the corner.

So many dreams came to die
on its dusty cushions,
a wilderness trying to be free
before the sky surrendered
to the hood of night.

I held the moon's hand
as we followed a disappearing road.
A woman was cleaning memory
with a sponge, and writing
a new assignment for tomorrow.

The days hung empty
on the calendar. Our task was
to fill the squares with
ambition, until we learned
to use the word hopeless.

THE PATH BEYOND KNOWLEDGE

It doesn't matter where you walk.
You will come upon a fence
holding back the unknown from
your gaze, your curious footsteps.
But if you go far enough,
a gap appears, a hole broken
through reality to reveal a green
and hidden enchantment.
There lies the uncreated world,
the realm of nameless eyes staring
at you from the dark. The silent
cries luring you to enter and be free.

A path leads to a spring, and a
house made of intangible wonders.
You are a child again, a wingless
half-angel barely touching the ground.
You have no past, and hardly know
how to picture your future, except
to paint it with your barely open eyes.
I've seen such flimsy images hanging
on the walls of a kindergarten once,
brush strokes that were uncertain
where to go, and circled back
to the garden standing forlorn
in the wilderness.

How we starve for a promise
from the parched silence

we are given at birth, and grow up
famished until the fence
appears, and dares us to
crawl again, on our knees,
into the mothering ignorance
whose breast we nurse from
in our calloused hands

NOVEMBER 5, 2024

I heard a woman sobbing in her
house and knocked. She answered
with red eyes and a damp rag
in her hands. She was embarrassed
to be found this way. She looked up
and asked what I wanted. Your tears,
I said. I want to soothe a weary nation.
I went away with a cup brimming
with her sorrow.

I heard a man sigh and lean against
his rake, and I asked what ailed him.
The pain in my heart, he said.
May I have it, I asked, holding out
my hand. Yes, but who would want
to feel my loneliness, he said.
But he gave me the crumbs
of his grief and I thanked him warmly.

A boy I knew from the neighborhood
was in a daze. He couldn't see his way.
Where are you headed, I asked.
Just home. So I guided him with my hand
and opened the door for him.
He gave me his broken eyes and went inside.
He had lost his dream, he said,
and didn't want to live.

The wounded were everywhere,
the broken souls standing with their
stooped shoulders and meth-eroded faces.
Something as wide as the sky
had fallen to the ground, and turned
to stone with our wasted prayers.

SEASONAL MISGIVINGS

I was hungry. I needed the sound
of a girl's voice calling to me from
a window, a breeze lugging summer
out of storage to hang once more
among the yew trees. I heard bagpipes
in the distance, the baleful laments
that goaded boys to their slaughter.
I pitied them. I wept into my sleeve
to think of so many dead buried
on the hillside. I wanted poetry
to sing so much more than it dared,
to curl its throat around each vowel
in an incantation over the innocent.
If love has pitched his mansion
in the place of excrement, then spring
grows out of the desert of the uterus.

III

WHERE BIRDS GO TO DIE

I used to listen to my blood
in a conch shell. It rushed over
the polished river stones
on its way to the sea. I heard
my first words uttered
from the crib, my cry for mama
hurled into the darkness
of the hall, the closed door.

Love kept walking away below
the window, not looking up
to see me staring at its shadow.
I heard breathing behind the door
but when I answered it, a ghost
was asking me for consolation.
I could only offer the kisses
I never felt in the middle
of the desert, just the sensation
of being wanted, then forgotten.

READING THE SKY FOR SIGNS

They say the hemline of a woman's skirt rises
and falls in some oblique relation
to the stock market, to the Dow Jones
Industrial Average, to the pulse in brokers' arms.
The glacial sludge of money has its intents
recorded by the bare legs of young women,
who walk gracefully on the pavements
of lower Manhattan. God bless them for it.

Meteors may also play a role in a tailors' shears,
how high they go in the soft, amorous
weave of cotton on the cusp of April,
when mating begins in earnest. The comets
that created us out of primordial dust
dropped their ashes into the salt
waves and vanished behind the sun, without
looking back at the blue iris growing
in the starkness of infinity. Tides pull at
the yearnings of young men, and lure them
into the sunlight to gaze at the future,
the fate that beguiles them.

Perhaps volcanoes sing their wonder
in tongues of magma.
At night the fires that trace the folds
of Atalanta's skirt foretell first kisses.
Let us praise the moon for its fickle chastity,
erotic one season, slivery and cold
in another, spurning one suitor after another

as the year staggers to its end.
The lute has a long memory and its strings
pluck at the fragile heart of every living thing.

The empty kitchen is all that's left of passion,
with its faucet dripping the same note
of despair into the sink at night.
A car comes to the door but no one answers.
A hat grows its veil of dust on the coat rack,
and whispers to a spider its tale of woe.
The old priest who came to administer last rites
is dead, and in his dismantled hands lies the remnants of a rosary.

BEIRUT IN AMBER

The dark blue water spread out
to the horizon, with the ruts
of an ancient road filled with
gold by the noon light. I smelled
mint and lemon from the tabouleh
heaped in a bowl
from which the men scraped up
mouthfuls with their pita spoons.
A cement skeleton was slowly rising
behind them, and the guttural
talk was fast and witty, as if work
were the first door of Eden.

The unpaved road led into town,
to Uncle Sam's bar, to the university
with its tiled roofs, the English-language
bookstore where my British war stories came from.
Shish kebab sweated on a spit,
the lamb giving off tangy parts of its soul
to the street, as men leaned forward
with their folded money ready in hand.

We milled around under Allah's gaze,
as boys ran alongside the trolleys
carrying a white woman's groceries
from the souk, their gaunt faces
eager to stay up with the grinding wheels.
Some ran bare foot, others made a tattoo

on the pavement with their flip flops.
These were the orphans of a wealthy city.

You couldn't count the times Beirut
was leveled by ancient foes.
The earth was layered with dead eras,
with the rubble of fantasies
and erotic tales of desert nights
among the hobbled camels, the goats
gazing around them as they chewed their memories.
All the towers fixed an unblinking gaze
on the sea, above the tethered falcons
muttering under leather hoods.

To grow up here, in the slow metronome
of the seasons, in the fretwork
of centuries carefully tuned to eternity,
was to know the emotions
of moths and flies, the tentative promises
life made to the ephemera of time.
Death was everywhere, buried under olive trees,
sequestered among the cracked limestone
of the hills, the inky shadows lying breathless
at the back of caves. Bedouins approached
on silent feet, plucking ouds
and singing through their slender noses.

Something as frail as a primrose
planted itself on this shelf of nowhere
and spread out in the bounty of the wells,
from which the city got its name. Bobbing
at the rim of the horizon were oil freighters
bound for the west, to swell the purses

of pampered burghers, the polished
bankers sliding in and out of limousines
as the day aged in its glass vase.

I broke my arm here, in the school's sand pit
learning how to do the western roll, a high jump.
I was just another anonymous butterfly
coming of age, reaching for my first flower,
my hunger for the scent of lilies
and the painful beauty of girls growing
out of their shells into womanhood.

THE END OF ELOISE

for Hilaire (1974-2023)

It was a stark sunny day
in July, a breeze blowing
back her hair on Lake Walk Street,
on the prairie slopes of central Texas.
She watched the man guide
the forks of his garbage truck
toward the dumpster, lift it
and angle it overhead to dump
the garbage into the maw
behind him. He was absorbed
with the task of not spilling anything.
He was already late to his daughter's
birthday party. He rushed a little.

She edged closer, put her foot
on the curb, and lowered herself
onto the pavement. Without
a thought she squeezed
behind the rear tires, until her back
arched against the muddy treads.
She felt her heart freeze, her pulse
turn to cement as she lay
still for thirty long seconds,
wondering if she would suddenly
spring up and run away. But she lay
there, in the dark of her mind,

in the throes of some nightmare
of inertia sludging through her veins.

Her husband had died a year ago,
tall and gaunt, with sunken cheeks
from years of battling brain cancer.
His withered flesh and burnt-out mind
had brought him to this crater on the moon,
where the night entombed him.
She couldn't bear it, walked out on him
and took a small apartment in a student complex.
No one was about. Not even a grackle
to rasp his jagged mating song.

The day was empty, a sudden desert
with the sun wasting its radiance
on the soft tar beneath her. She lay
on her side, until the gears reversed
and began to move. She was nudged,
and then caught in the mouth of gravity.
Life had cheated her again.
Her father dead, her kids no longer
waiting for her at home, but off
on their own pointless journeys.
She could leave now, having
left a note to each of them, an envelope
full of cash, a neatly packed suitcase.

She was Eloise to her beloved Abelard,
the bright spirts of this age. She was
meant to soar, to illuminate the dark
past of Spain, to lift the lid of its spirits

and hidden wisdom, to breathe the air
of this sunny morning into the corners
of a lost world. She felt her head
suddenly collapse in a flood of heat,
her shoulders to fold like paper
against her spine, her last breath
escaping into the arcanum of Quixote's dust.

WHATEVER HAPPENED TO SUMMER?

Shadows come and go
like bewildered ghosts
trying to find the door
to eternity. There is none.
Only the sun pouring
down out of a frail sky
at the threshold of winter,
as if the floor were Eden
and light was a worn-out shovel.

I've been lost before. I searched
my room for a sock once,
and could only find a shoe
I had thrown away long ago.
It wanted to walk again.
It was tired of being in the dark.
It hated the silence, the idleness
of solitude, the shredded reality
of a mind without visions.

A girl asked me to kiss her
on her doorstep, as we stood
in the halo of a street light.
Her face was an invitation
to journey into the far side
of communion, where the soul
aches to be merged with otherness.
I merely brushed her lips
and walked home, empty.

This is the country of lost causes.
The houses are dark with unkept
promises, with conversation left
broken at the moment of truth.
The basement cannot climb
to the attic to reclaim its experience.
The past keeps slipping away
undetected by the dust, by the rusting
bikes and piles of old clothes.

I am ashamed of my mortality,
as if growing old were an affront
to the mountains, the rivers flowing
into the mouth of forever.
My faith evaporates like April rain,
until the parched granite rises
and declares its freedom from change.
I lie down to comfort it, and feel
the cold, aloof refusal to be loved.

WALKING WITH WALT WHITMAN'S GHOST

I've fallen behind a crowd
of commuters going home
after a long day. No one talks.
We are all watching the pavement
give beneath us. The city
looms overhead like the vaults
of a giant bridge. I see shadows
forming in pockets of sunset,
in the first fingerprints of night.

Lights go on, the suburbs
reach out to me as I pass by,
lonely lights inviting me
to dinner, to sit and watch
TV with the family, to go to bed
in the cavernous emptiness
of the bedroom. A car makes
music with its lisping pistons
as it passes by, a bus wheezes
with emphysema as it lunges
uphill with smoke in its lungs.

I try to make friends but
everything is closed and dark,
and I am the last human being
awake to see miracles
tumbling from the sky, showering
us with promises.

IV

BLUES ON AN UNTUNED GUITAR

The burnished crests of far off hills
make afternoon into an antique store.
The silver on the shelves has not
been polished in a generation.
The sky is full of the anticipation of winter.

Even the wind is fleeing south
to embrace the glinting waves.
I've been waiting for an hour
for the bus, until someone
tells me they no longer come this way.

I smell coffee brewing, but it's
just a burnt wind that lost its way.
I taste hope but it's a page torn from a diary.
The earth spins like a roulette wheel
trying to stop on a bright tomorrow.

WHAT THE CALENDAR TELLS US

The dead whisper our names
as we pass by the graveyard
where time gives up the past.
Even the stones melt, the trees
grow old and wither up
like skeletons, the shrill cries
of children disappear into the woods.

This is the month boys stumble
into manhood, gripping
the gate post before shouldering
their duty to be brave.
It's the breeze bringing the breath
of girls into the open, where
lovers are eager to propose.

It's the door that falls open
tonight, to the tedious weakness
of a floor lamp burning
in the corner of a living room.

HOW WE FAIL

I'm watching the maple trees across
the street, drying my hair after a shower.
The leaves are falling, faster and faster,
covering the ground with mosaics
of gold and red tiles, as if this were
the foyer of a brothel.
The leaves escape the mother tree
without regret, as if
they belonged to some unfinished
tale about the failure of summer
to build a lasting monument.

The writer came back from his nap
and saw the flaws in his thinking,
the gaps he left yawning with hunger
for insight, for courage to say
he couldn't imagine another world,
an unreal paradise where permanence
loved the sunshine, the scent of roses,
the passing warmth and laughter
of a girl on her way to school.
He couldn't make his logic rip
open the husk of vision
hidden behind words, the syllables
that spelled out a new utopia.

He lies down to comfort his misery,
to hold himself like a mother calming
a child's fall in the yard.

The bicycle lay there, mangled by gravity,
spokes curled up out of the wheel rim.
He was an orphan in the world, the writer
without a god, without an angel
to lead him through the caverns of dread
to some stairway hidden in the shadows,
some desolate steps curving around
a center that held up all the doubts of the world.

QUESTIONS I POSE TO YOU

Who composed great music after Beethoven?
It's like trying to write a pure line of poetry
without adjectives, without too many nouns,
just the luster of verbs glowing in a beet garden.

You must shiver off the clutter of the mind,
the self-concealing language of
timidity. No one wants to know how you really feel,
or why you are hesitating to go your way.

Candor was lost after the Middle Ages,
when God inhabited the act of shelling beans,
shucking the ears, lugging milk to the market,
shooing lambs away from the millet sack.

No one inhabits what they create, anymore.
The wilting roses have no one to till the soil
and water them; rain will have to do the work.
The temples stand empty, the landscape barren.

I love you turns to mush after the first kiss.
Fondling is the desolate act of loneliness;
it makes the hands useless to hold
the sanctity of someone in your arms.

WHEN THE STORM CAME

When the storm came, everyone
trembled at its anger, its power
to wipe away the human world.
No one dared to yell at the sky
or rage against the wilderness.

Instead, they huddled in church.
They knelt down to pray, to hold hands
as the wind blew down
the trees, ate the last shreds of light
falling out of a broken heaven.

A girl cried in her mother's arms.
A dog barked in the corner.
Someone offered the blind man
a dollar to buy his faith in God.
No one could go home again.

Fires licked at their memories,
swallowing the monuments of the past.
Language crumbled in their hands,
as vision dissolved into
make believe and slowly died.

PROMISES MADE AT BED TIME

Sometimes a street is not a street.
It's a page out of a discarded book,
the one your mother read to you
before bed time. You were drifting
into the twilight of your table lamp,
ready to dream that you lived
in a gloomy castle with an old dog.

Words entered you, one by one,
promising a brighter life, a green
hill full of apple trees, a wheel barrow
freshly painted in the shade of a barn,
the river brimming with fallen
rain flowing below you. The sentences
were like fingers reaching the edge
of your sheet and tugging at your feet.

A road was being invented before you,
a path that led out of your knowledge
into the silky darkness of night,
where stars were hanging the light
of so many diamonds. The world
was being born again, rewriting itself
into a fairy tale where you roamed
at the edge of childhood. Everything
was possible, waiting for you.

You only had to stop and ask a question.
But it took all the courage you had
and more, and you rode on, weeping
at your cowardice, praying you were
someone else, and that the road
was taking you into adulthood.
You could feel the pain of first love
hiding its face behind the door,
knowing you must knock twice
to taste the bitterness you longed for.

LIKE NOAH'S RAVEN

The moon hangs over the dead garden.
The only voice to hear is the crying
of an owl in the blackened cemetery.
Winter kisses the tombs with frozen lips
and holds its spirits in her withered arms.

Night erases the rumors of last summer,
the shy laughter, glances that raced
through the heart like bumble bees,
the pulse that unraveled in the soul
when the first cold wind arrived.

Look, says my wife, as she points
to a bug crawling up the window.
It was a sign, like Noah's raven,
come back from dry land after
the world lay drowned in an angry sea.

Miracles happen, even after slaughter,
after a thousand Gazas lay in ruins.
A rose unwinds from a hidden spool
and opens its blood-red petals,
one by one. And then a butterfly appears.

What had disintegrated into dust,
into ashes, rubble-filled craters,
into broken streets and howling doorways,
resurrects itself on the power
of a grieving voice and a forgiving mind.

THE SIX O'CLOCK NEWS

Loneliness remembers everything.
You walk down an empty street
and your childhood looms before you,
a vast portrait of your troubled
face, hands reaching out to the air
without hope, only a stranger staring
out of a window to your left.

At the pier, the sea crumples up
like a love letter you never sent.
It lies there at the bottom of reality,
a fragile relic of a vanished civilization.
The store where you bought your first
Valentine closed its doors one winter afternoon
and no one ever rented the space again.

Even the school house is dark. The rooms
are crammed with old sewing machines
for migrants to learn a new trade.
They plied their worn out fingers
trying to thread a needle, but the ruins
of a village were still smoking in their eyes.
A train whistle dies in the twilight.

WHEN FALL TURNS THE MAPLES RED

The wind disappears down a dark hallway.
No one knows where storms begin or end,
only that trees bow and perform
their dances on an empty stage.

Overhead, a famished sky slides
down the glimmering twilight.
Even the glare from the window
fails to illuminate the white ground.
Laundry fades in the dark,
like the pages of a photo album.

Why is love so cruel to the heart?
A car roams down the wrong road
in search of a house, which lies
among the charred ruins of a fire.
Listen and you will hear the emptiness
talking to itself, slurring its words.

A COLD AND EMPTY HOUSE

The mountains slumber in amnesia.
Blank minds at ease in the brittle
granite beds, the creeks turning
to mush as they rub against the snow.
Memory has buried its diary under
the glass lid of late November.

My heart is knitting wool in its creaky
fingers, with the floor humming
a monotonous tune as I rock.
The air is gray with a dust of old facts
and rumors, the worn-out fear of wars
that never blossomed into violence.

The playground down the street
is alive with the shrill cries of boys
fighting for the ball. They stand tensely
around the tether pole and wait
to punch the ball into higher orbit,
to keep it safe until it returns to
their greedy hands, only to be liberated
again into the knife-sharp air.

This is my theory of money I keep
trying to publish in a magazine.
But my envelope always comes back
to taunt me into finding another stamp
and punching my thoughts once more
into flight. Inertia gently lowers every
escaping wish back down to earth
to lie among the other rusting cries.

IRREDUCIBLE THINGS

To grow old is to think away
the clutter of experience,
to be in emptiness
with only a chair to sit on,
and a light to measure
the boundless realm of nothing.

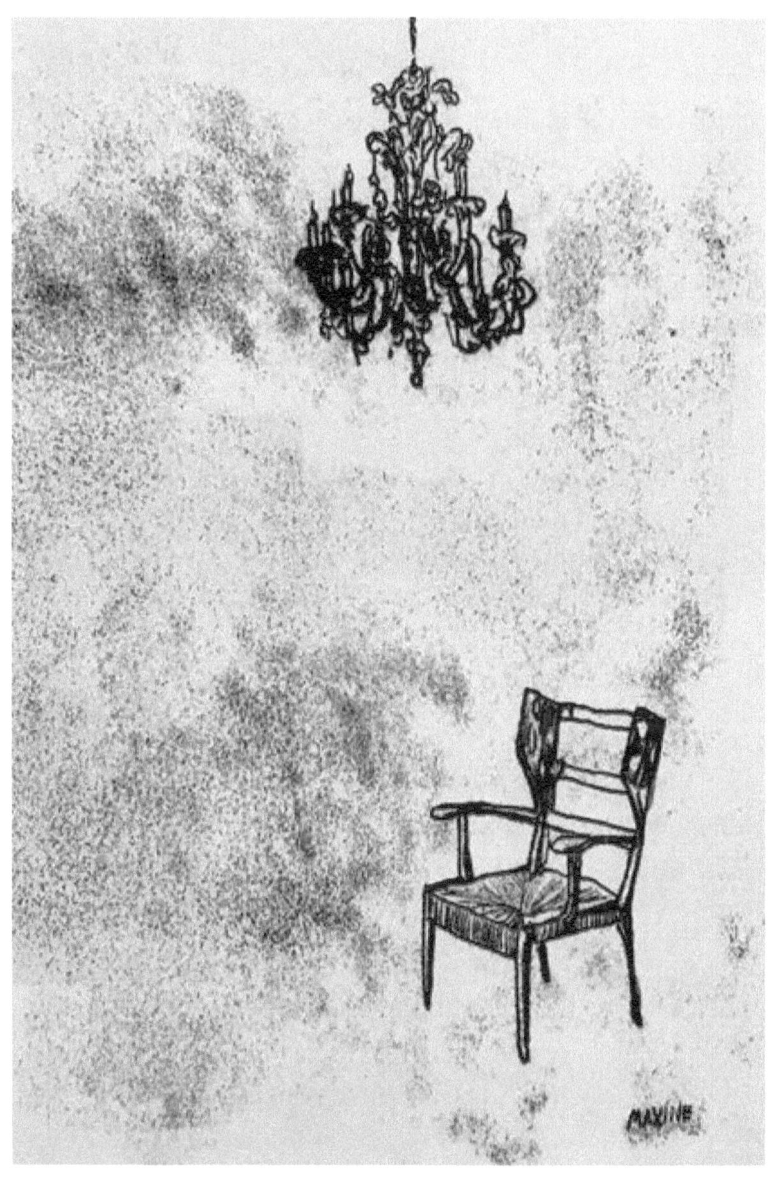

PLAYING BOULES

Iron balls roll in space
like planets, wobbling
over ruts and warps
as if escaping time.
But gravity conquers
chance without apology.

What human being doesn't
long to toss a world
into flight, to break
the barrier of reason
holding back the dream world?
Especially at night.

WHY WE CANNOT SLEEP AT NIGHT

An island of pure light
floats on the water
where hope creates
a paradise as thin as air.

THE PIANO TEACHER

No! No! No! he said
banging the lid of the piano shut.
You are trying to play music
without a soul. You have no
spirit to guide you, no
feeling that there is a path
through the chaos toward heaven.

Genius is pure vision, a god-sense
that makes the clutter disappear
as you step forward through
the marsh grass, and put your foot
delicately into the sodden earth.
The echoes of mere voices
simply add to the clatter of existence.
You are repeating mere noise
in every other note. Listen,
the echoes linger, the trash of existence
hangs in the air, even now.

Do you remember the first time
you kissed a girl's lips
and felt her breath enter
you, a breath so sweet you were dizzy
with the scent of roses?
And the garden was whirling
in an orbit of perfect silence,
until the bees came and hummed
you into a trance of ecstasy?

That's the music you cannot play.
You have no ear to tune, no
heart to quicken you into prayer
with your fingers poised over
the keys, no hunger for purity
hidden under the veil
of human desire. I'm sorry
for you. You have youth, you
are handsome, your profile
is as fine as a knife slicing bread.
But your hands hold up mere
dough, not manna. The field
was not your angel, my friend.
You were given the crumbs
of creation, the dirt and the stones
of the orphaned world, not
the escape of a god from mortality.

I can't teach you how to believe
I couldn't teach myself. I am Cain
lost in the desert of decaying flesh,
the waste land of imperfection
and selfish desires, the rain
that pours into the soul
and fills it with self-doubt. I am
scarred with my mortal sins
and roam the wilderness looking
for a saint to cleanse me.
Play me Chopin to see if there
is not a fragment of light
left among the rubbish.